Meetings

and

Sales Presentations

Part Four

SALES TRAINING

Wayne E Shillum – Author

WES MARKETING

MEETINGS

AND

SALES PRESENTATIONS

Wayne E Shillum – Author

WES MARKETING

DEDICATION

This Part is Dedicated to Everyone

Who Insisted on having a Meeting

For Everything you could Possibly Think of

It often seemed Anything Could Trigger

These Words

"WE NEED TO HAVE A MEETING"

But they All were

Invaluable Training for Use in my Career

When it Became My Turn to hold and run Meetings

And make Sales Presentations.

Thanks to All!

Table of Contents

INTRODUCTION

Selling is all about Communicating

The need to communicate will take place before you even step outside of your office to visit your prospects, clients, or peers. The need starts within the walls of your own company and involves everyone you work with.

Without establishing a solid base of communication within your own company, you will not achieve the full potential of selling success outside of it.

In sales; as in life, you are very much controlled by how well you convey the messages you want to deliver to those around you.

It is not only what you are thinking and are able to convey effectively to others; but also, how well you interpret what others are transmitting in their actions and words back to you.

In Sales

The learned ability part of communicating well with others is often overlooked. Many sales people take this skill for granted and never reach their full potential.

Often it will take a determined effort by sales people to improve their ability to communicate and make effective sales presentations.

Learning and fine tuning their communication skills will greatly improve their selling ability and increase their closing percentages.

These skills are essential when meeting with prospects and associates.

Areas where you rely on being able to Communicate Effectively

- Your office co-workers
- Your Prospects who are yet to become Clients
- Your New and Existing clients,
- Your Suppliers
- Your peers in the industry

From the initial prospecting stages, right through all your meetings with your prospects, your presentations, closing the sale and answering objections; communication is an essential part of selling.

Today we have many ways to convey our thoughts.

- Land lines, mobile telephones and other mobile devices
- Faxes, emails, post office, videos, You Tube
- Conferencing, webinars, podcasts,
- Skype – the online face to face meetings,
- In person face to face meetings.

Most of your meetings and sales presentations will be greatly enhanced by perfecting your communication skills.

The Different Types of Meetings

- Your initial introductory meetings,
- Your fact-finding meetings
- Your dress rehearsal presentations
- The final meetings for sales presentations and quotations.
- The Call Back Meeting

Your Challenges

Before you venture into the actual world of selling you must learn how to put successful sales presentations together and deliver them.

Unless you develop communicating skills to their fullest potential, your sales presentations will have little or only mediocre successes.

Successful meetings do not just happen. They are planned and structured with all the essential elements. They are rehearsed over and over until they can be delivered with perfection.

COMMUNICATION

The Overview

As we said in our introduction, most people do not give the area of communication much thought in their day to day lives, so it is very understandable why its importance is often overlooked in the sales profession.

We have three levels of communicating available and studies show that 100% of successful communicating is made up of all three of these areas. (We will refer to them as Levels)

We will list them in order of how most people place their importance and use them when they convey their messages to one another. We will also indicate by percentage how these studies view their overall effectiveness.

Level One – Content

Content in the words we choose and use; mostly in our written words (advertising) but also the content of our spoken dialogue".

Studies say Level One accounts for only 7% of the potential for communication success.

Level Two – Voice Toning

Our Voice and the way we say it makes a difference. Studies say voice tones account for 38% of our potential ability in communicating.

Level Three – Body Language

Facial and Body Movement – Our eyes, mouth, head, arms and legs account for the greatest portion at 55% of our ability to communicate with others.

Above Figures from studies by: Dr. Albert Mehrabian Professor Emeritus at UCLA. **"The Essence of Communication"**
When we look at the results of the studies made by **Dr. Albert Mehrabian,** we begin to understand why most of the sales efforts fail in communicating with others.

What you can Expect (based on these studies)

- 7% is accessed - when Sales People send or drop off literature and hope for a call from the client.
    - 93% of their potential effectiveness which are (Levels 2 & 3) will still be unused.
- 38% additional potential can be accessed - If they are able to talk to the person by telephone.
    - Now a total of 45% has been accessed if they combine content with voice delivery.
    - 55% is still untouched in Level 3.

This does not mean that they will be 45% effective, as no effort is perfect. Their effectiveness will be determined by how well they are able to perform the skills of creating content and talking on the telephone.

Many sales are made using these two levels alone, without a face to face meeting. Telemarketing sales is a prime example.

Add a Face-to-Face Meeting

Seeing the prospect in person provides access to the final and largest part of communication. This is the 55% that one can add using *Body Language* to communicate.

This body language feature occurs in both presenting your offerings and in observing the client's reaction to your presentation.

In most prospecting, our goal is to arrange a face to face meeting so that we can present our company and its offerings using all three levels of communication.

Here we will find out the full extent of their needs and interest for our products or services.

Telephone Sales

Some direct sales companies use just the telephone to make their sales. Here they are accessing only content and voice to get the sale.

The need to do these two areas well is very important, as a sale depends on achieving one's goal by accessing only 45%.

These telemarketing companies develop very effective methods in the use of these two levels. They are great places to learn and develop these first two levels of communication.

For the rest of the direct selling methods, we use these first two areas (content and voice tone), to qualify and arrange a meeting in person. At this meeting, we can make use of all three levels of communication when we make our first face-to-face presentation.

Again, this in-person meeting does not mean we are able to have 100% effective communications results but, we have access to 100 percent of the process.

It only means the opportunity is there to use all three levels. The results are up to you and how well you develop these skills.

Rate your Present Communication Skills

CONTENT - or promotional material

Rate your ability from 0 to 7% =?

VOICE - delivery of your message

Rate your ability from 0 to 38% =?

BODY LANGUAGE - when talking

Rate your ability from 0 to 55% =?

Total out of 100% =?

For the average person, it would optimistically be as follows:

1.	Content -	2 – 4%	average – 3%
2.	Voice -	10 – 15%	average – 12%
3.	Body Language -	19 – 23%	average – 21%
	Normal Result is -	**31 to 42%**	**average – 36%**

If this is an optimistic level of communications for most people to reach without any type of training, why do sales people limit themselves to only a 31 to 42% (36% average) chance of success?

Without Training in Communication Skills

Just sending or dropping literature off to introduce yourself is only 7% of your Prospecting Job. One might reach 4%. If there is a real need, sometimes this will create interest in your product or service, but why not improve your chances.

A telephone call by you and a brief conversation gives you a much-improved opportunity and adds another 38% potential in your prospecting efforts. One might add up to another 15%

You need an in-person meeting to access all your communication capabilities. Optimistically one might add 23%

This is where you will have employed all three parts of the communication capabilities.

Do you want to be limited to 31% or even 42%? I hope not.

Many sales people send or drop off literature and feel that they have done their prospecting job. They are just getting started. It is important to use all three areas to complete their full prospecting responsibilities.

The goal is to make the most out of each communicating area and get as close to the 100% level as you can.

Level One - The Words

Content

The words you use; both spoken and in your visual aids, is where it all begins. Selection of the right words to use should be a priority.

Unfortunately for many; little attention is given here, and as a result the limits are pre-set on how much can be achieved in all three levels.

Using great content allows you to create interest and optimize all three levels of communicating when they take place. With your content and words, you can create a powerful format that delivers a clear focused message to your prospect.

You will have the foundation to add emphasis with your voice tones and body language to optimum levels.

Without great content, you have already limited your chances for success.

Key Points for Content

1. Have a great Opening.
2. Provide Key Points that will Create and Hold Interest.
3. Use words that allow optimum use of all three levels
4. Provide a compelling Closing or “Call-to-Action”

USE CONTENT - or words that provide optimum possibilities

- Use words that are POWERFULL and allow you to use your voice and body to emphasize them.
- Use words that are PRECISE and are not just fillers or close substitutes of what you should be using.
- Use words that will provide a CLEAR and FOCUSED message.
- **Use words** that will create the desire to act.
- Use words that will MOTIVATE.
- Use words that will allow you to convey ENTHUSIASM.

Add words that Convey Emotion.

Use words that will convey HAPPINESS, SUCCESS and PLEASURE in the use your products or services.

Use a Thesaurus to access synonyms that achieve all the above.

Content is the first part of the communication process and it is what will allow you to do the rest effectively. In the preparation of your written material you should use all the support areas available to you.

Most writing programs have a spell and grammar check so there should be no excuse for misspelled words or bad grammar.

- Misspelled words can seriously detract from what could be a great article or presentation.
- Omitting Punctuation can lead to loss of clarity and will result in confusion.
- **A thesaurus** can be found in most writing programs.

This allows you to select powerful and accurate words for your descriptions and explanations; while avoiding repetition of the same word.

This allows you to provide clear and focused messages that are not boring to read or listen to.

A dictionary should never be far from your reach. The use of the wrong word in your narrative efforts can have disastrous results. It will cause the loss of attention and credibility.

Other people's quotes may be used on various topics to get your point across. This is often more compelling than your own words and these quotes can often add validity and can say it exactly to suit the occasion.

Preparation

The time to get it right, is in the initial preparation process for your first contact with the prospect. It starts with the content for the spoken word.

You should always make use of this very valuable *"time of preparation"* at the beginning to get it right; so, you can say it right.

Accurate, powerful and descriptive messaging creates the ability for you to add emphasis with voice tones and body language.

The written word is a permanent record for all to see and re-visit

Having the right content allows you to leave the right message to be viewed over and over.

Your written words will also remind your prospect of the key points and benefits of your products or services after your presentation becomes history.

Take Time to Prepare

And

You will be on Your Way

To Becoming a Great Communicator

Level Two - Voice Tones

Making Voice Presentations

Your voice is your trademark. It is your main identifying feature when you are making presentations or just talking in general.

Your Voice Must Consistently Sound:

1. Upbeat and Positive
2. Warm and Friendly
3. Under Control
4. Authoritative
5. Clear

Smiling will automatically warm up the tone of your voice and your audience will notice the difference even if they cannot see you.

Research done by the department of Psychology at the University of Pittsburgh USA; indicated that people make distinctive judgments of others based on the tone of the speaker's voice.

Specifically, that a Deeper Voice Tone

Creates more Authority and Credibility

Everyone has a voice range, so it would be good to practice the lower end of your voice range, to deliver better presentations.

Try speaking at different levels that are comfortable to use.

Your voice will influence people and can often imply the amount of knowledge that you have. This also increases your degree of professionalism and will increase your closing percentages.

If you want to be a credible authority about your presentation, voice tone is an important factor.

People Respond

Either Negatively or Positively

To *"Voice Tone"*

Practice by recording your voice at different levels and listen to the results. Keep trying until you reach the right level. Get feedback from your friends and peers.

Negative Reactions to Voice Tone

A shrill or high-pitched voice tends to have a negative impact on an audience. They will find the high pitch irritating. These presenters are often perceived to lack authority and knowledge of their topic.

They lose the Interest and Attention of the Audience.

A Monotone has little or no variance in energy levels emitted. It tends to become instantly boring to the audience and is very dysfunctional in presentations.

People usually disengage quickly and very little; if anything, is accomplished by the speaker.

Speaking Fast - It is also normal for people to speak faster when delivering a presentation. This is very dangerous. Keep it slow enough for your client to easily follow your train of thought.

There is a definite need to speak slower to allow people to digest what you are saying. People who speak fast are felt to be confusing, and less intelligent.

Things that Create a Positive Reaction

A varied tone rising and falling allows you to emphasize your words and phrases.

Emotions like enthusiasm, humor, excitement, sorrow and concern are all conveyed by different tone levels as they inject different forms of energy into your words.

There is also a distinct difference between a person hearing what has been said, and a person understanding what has been said.

- Hearing is automatic. It takes very little or no effort.
- Understanding is not automatic. It takes a lot more effort and concentration.

Understanding is the act of focusing one's mind on what is being said to grasp its meaning. Not only is it good to speak slower but pausing between key points, will also allow information to sink in.

Slowing down and pausing will also give you more time to select your upcoming tone levels and gestures.

People who speak slower are perceived to be more intelligent and thoughtful. The implication is that they are thinking about what they are saying.

Examples of Reactions

How we speak does influence others and the following *"situation questions"* indicate how we express ourselves in different circumstances.

Situation Questions

- How do you greet a friend that you have not seen for years?
- How do you speak to someone who has just experienced a death in the family?
- How do you speak when you are angry, excited or sad?
- If you are scolding someone or calling out because they are in harm's way, how are your voice deliveries at these times?

Everyone can Improve

The way they Deliver their Message

Listen to the announcers on the radio. Listen to politicians, as they are usually the masters of voice deliverance.

Record Yourself and Listen.

Adjust your delivery until you are happy and comfortable with the new and improved presenter.

When making your presentation standing provides the greatest range of communication possibilities. It allows the full use of the entire body to express yourself.

It also allows you to breathe deeply and add more power to your voice levels.

Often it is a sit-down meeting by client choice, but you will still have many options available. Sit erect, shoulders back, chest slightly out and breath from the diaphragm.

Before your presentation, it is good to drink some water to lubricate your vocal cords. If it is a long presentation try to have a glass of water handy.

Level Three - Body Language

Our Information Sources

Charles Darwin was the first one to bring forth this information in his book titled *"The Expressions of the Emotions in Man and Animals"* Published in 1872.

Paul Ekman - a Californian psychiatrist in the 1960's; and an expert in facial expressions along with **Sorenson and Friesen,** conducted and published the results of extensive studies with a variety of peoples and world cultures.

Their Studies Also Confirmed

Darwin was Right

When people think of sales, often very little attention is given to using body language to improve the results.

Even though it makes up 55% of the potential effective communicating skills, it is still given the least consideration when people are making presentations.

The Four Levels of Body Communication

We will examine Body Communication from four areas.

1. Face and Head
2. Hands Arms and Legs
3. Body Positioning
4. Personal Space

When these four areas are combined, their effectiveness is greater than the sum of the individual parts. We can create even more powerful messaging, when these areas work in harmony.

1. Face and Head

Facial Expressions

There are 6 universal Facial expressions that are used and recognized in their ability to convey certain human emotions.

The 6 Expressions are:

1) Happiness
2) Sadness
3) Fear
4) Disgust
5) Surprise
6) Anger

They are:

Universally recognized

Human evolved

Genetically inherited

Not dependent on social learning or one's environment

Studies worldwide indicate that these emotions are recognized regardless of culture and educational background.

By using these facial expressions, we can transcend cultures and language barriers and can get an emotional feeling understood without the utterance of a single word.

Facial expressions can play a very important role and can often create subtle reactions that improve your message when used in the proper way.

1. Eye Communication

Our eyes are a very important part of the non-verbal signals that we send to others. It is often said that you can see into a person's sole by observing their eyes. It is also said that the eyes do not lie.

To a certain extent, we all tend to be able to read people's eyes without knowing how or why. It seems to be an ability that we are born with.

We can also see whether another person's eyes are focused on us or not. (often indicating if they are listening or interested)

We can Easily Detect the Difference of:

- A Glazed Over lost or Confused look
- A Blank stare suggesting their thoughts are somewhere else
- An awkward or secret glance - often done in an embarrassing situation

- The prelude to a teary eye warning us of things to come

Just look at our eyelids, and the ability to widen and close our eyes. We also can enlarge or contract our pupils and move our eyes about.

It is no surprise of the extent at which our eyes can convey a wide variety of messages.

The importance in conveying a feeling or an emotion during the deliverance of your presentation is equally as important as getting a direct reading on what is being felt by your audience in return.

The following will show what is normally meant as it relates to the person who is giving the signals and making the movements.

The designation of right or left pertains to the person who is giving the signal. When someone is speaking, and left eye is stated, it means their left eye.

Of course, when you are listening, watching or facing these people their left is on your right side. The following left/right designations refer to the Speaker's left or right.

What the eyes are saying

When the eyes look

RIGHT AND UP – The person is imagining, fabricating.

LEFT AND UP – They are recalling or remembering.

When the person looks sideways

RIGHT – They are imagining sounds.

RIGHT AND DOWN – They are assessing feelings.

LEFT – They are remembering sounds.

LEFT AND DOWN – They are usually rationalizing or self-talking.

When eyes make direct Contact

WHEN SPEAKING: – The person is showing honesty.

WHEN LISTENING: – The person is listening and attentive.

WIDENING OF EYES SHOWS – Interest, appeal

RUBBING OF EYES SHOWS – Disbelief upset or is bored

AN EYE SHRUG – Shows frustration.

EYEBROWS RISING – Greeting or recognition

EYEBROW FLASH SHOWS – Indicates acknowledgment.

2. Mouth Communication

The mouth acts independently and smiling is a big part of body language, as is frowning and pouting.

The mouth can be open wide, closed tight or any position in between. Each provides a unique expression and meaning.

The mouth is associated with many body language signals. The mouth can be covered by one's hands or fingers, and it plays a central part in one's facial expressions.

The mouth has more moving parts than any other sensory organ; therefore, it provides almost unlimited variables of expression.

What the Mouth is Saying When

TIGHT LIPPED – Withheld feelings

TWISTED SMILE – Mixed feelings or sarcasm

DROPPED JAW SMILE – Is considered a faked smile.

MOUTH OPEN HANDS AT SIDE - Shows surprise.

BOTTOM LIP JUTTING OUT - Upset, Flirting

BITING LIP – Shows tenseness.

SMILE HEAD TILTED UP – Playfulness, teasing, coy

GENUINE LAUGH – Indicates relaxation.

A FORCED LAUGH – Signals nervousness.

GRINDING TEETH – Shows anger.

HAND OVER MOUTH – Shows shock, suppression holding back.

Head Communication

The head tends to lead and determine general body direction and is used in directional likes and dislikes.

The head is very flexible it can turn, project forward, withdraw, tilt sideways, tilt forwards and tilt backwards.

These Movements have Different Meanings

When our hands interact with our head we achieve very powerful body language.

What the Head is Saying When

HEAD NODDING – Shows agreement.

SLOW HEAD NODDING – Attentive listening

FAST HEAD NODDING – Impatient, hurry up

HEAD HELD UP – Alertness neutrality

HEAD HELD HIGH – Superiority, arrogant

HEAD IS FORWAND UPRIGHT – Interest, positive reaction

HEAD TILTED DOWN – Criticism, admonishment

HEAD TILTED TO ONE SIDE - Non-threatening, submissive, thoughtful

HEAD SHAKING SIDE TO SIDE – Disagreement

PROLONGED HEAD SHAKING – Strong disagreement

HEAD DOWN IN RESPONSE – Negative, discontented, unhappy

HEAD DOWN WHILE PERFORMING ACTIVITY – Defeated, tired

CHIN UP – Pride, defiant, confidence

2. Hands Arms and Legs

1. Hand Communication

Body language involving hands is extensive. They are expressive and flexible tools and convey a lot of conscious signaling. When the hands are combined with the other parts of the body, there is usually a signal.

What our Hands Are Saying When

BOTH PALMS HELD HIGH AND FACING OUT – Is Defensive

ONE PALM IN FRONT FACING OUT –This means to stop.

HAND ON HEART – Seeking to be believed, allegiance

When

PALMS LOWERED FACING UP OPEN – Truthful, honesty, appealing submissive. Asking for a response

PALMS DOWN MOVING UP AND DOWN FINGERS SPREAD – Asking to calm down in a group

PALMS DOWN – Shows authority, strength, or dominance.

PALMS UP, THEN DOWN, REPEATED – Striving for an answer

When

FINGERS POINTING - Aggression, threat, emphasis

FINGER POINT IN AIR – Creates Emphasis.

FINGER SIDE TO SIDE – Indicates a Warning, or a refusal.

FINGER UP AND DOWN – Admonishment, emphasis

FINGER POINTING AND NODDING WITH SMILE – Acknowledgment

CLENCHED FISTS – Resistance, aggression, determination

HAND CHOP – Strong emphasis

When

THUMBS POINTED DOWN – Shows disapproval or rejection.

INDEX FINGER AND THUMB TOUCHING AT TIPS SAME HAND – Indicates approval. It's OK.

THUMBS POINTED UP – Means approval, OK

THUMBS CLENCHED INSIDE FISTS – Self comforting, insecurity

RUBBING HANDS TOGETHER – Shows anticipation

PINCHING RUBBING NOSE WHEN LISTENING – Thoughtfulness, waiting

REMOVING GLASSES – Alerting, wishing to speak

When

HAND SUPPORTING CHIN OR SIDE of FACE - Evaluation, tired, sad, bored

TWO FINGERED V PALMS INWARD – Offensive or contempt

TWO FINGERED V PALMS OUTWARD – Victory or peace

INTERWOVEN CLENCHED FINGERS – Frustration, negativity or anxiousness

HAND CLASPING WRIST – Frustration

CHIN RESTING ON THUMB INDEX FINGER POINTING UP -Evaluation, I am thinking.

When

HANDS STROKING CHIN – Thoughtfulness

TOUCHING SCRATCHING NOSE WHEN SPEAKING – Lying, exaggerate

NECK SCRATCHING – Doubt, disbelief

HANDS IN POCKETS – Disinterest, boredom

HANDS CLASPING HEAD – Shows a calamity.

HANDS OVER EARS – Rejection, resistance

FINGER TIPS AND THUMBS TOUCHING EACH OTHER ON OPPOSITE HANDS PUSHING TOGETHER AND POINTING UPWARDS –Indicates thoughtfulness, looking for answers or Deep thinking.

The Handshake

The Hand shake evolved from ancient times as a gesture of trust by showing that no weapon was being held by the outstretched arm.

The handshake has developed into a social process of greeting or saying goodbye and showing friendship. It is often used in business to signify that a transaction has been agreed to. It is sometimes used as a way of judging character; but here, it is not always accurate.

What the Handshake is Usually Saying

When handshakes are uncomfortably firm they can display disrespect or appear to be phony and are faking affection. When they are, weak and feel like a damp rag, the person is judged to be weak and uncertain.

Different interpretations will occur in cultures where hand shaking is not a normal greeting and may not follow the same interpretation.

What the Position says when

HANDSHAKE PALMS DOWN – Shows dominance

HANDSHAKE PALMS UP – Shows submission accommodating

EQUAL AND VERTICLE – Non-threatening

When

HANDSHAKE USES BOTH HANDS - Seeking to convey trustworthiness honesty - Seeking to control

IT IS PUMPUNG – Shows Enthusiasm

IT IS WEAK – Varies maybe shows weakness or submission

IT IS FIRM – Outward confident

CLASPING THE OTHER PERSONS ARM - Seeking control

There is much more significance to handshaking than most people realize. Politicians know this only too well and often go to great lengths to be on the appropriate side during a press conference or during meetings.

Positioning Signals

If the person they are greeting is on their left during the handshake when facing the audience or camera, their hand is on top of a handshake demonstrating they are dominant.

Their hand will be facing down while the other person's hand will be on the bottom facing up.

The variables of using one or both arms and hands also will imply dominance or submission. The use of both arms and hands implies control.

Observe Politicians

As an interesting exercise, the next time you watch when politicians or dignitaries greet each other; observe their body language.

Watch especially heads of countries greeting each other on camera. See if they are maneuvering to be on the dominant side with their hand on top and palms facing down, as seen by their audience.

Also watch to see who Clasps the other persons Arm.

They all know the implications of this positioning and it can be quite humorous sometimes to watch the efforts made to be on the appropriate side.

2. Arms Communication

Arms act as defensive barriers when across the body. When they are open, they demonstrate openness.

Arms clearly indicate moods and feelings especially when combined with other parts of the body.

What the Arms Are Saying

CROSSED ARMS – Shows a defensive position or uncertainty.

CROSSED ARMS AND CLENCHED FISTS – Hostile, defensive

CROSSED AND GRIPPING UPPER ARMS – Insecurity

ARMS BEHIND BODY HANDS CLASPED – Confidence, authority

ARMS OPEN – Openness "hello world"

PLAYING IMAGINARY VIOLIN – Shows mock sympathy or sadness.

3. Legs and Feet

The body language of legs and feet is more difficult to control consciously than are other body parts.

Often it will provide good clues to one's true feelings, because of this fact.

There are also definite differences between men and women due to cultural orientation.

Leg signals are often supported by corresponding arm signals such as crossed arms and legs signifying detachment disinterest rejection or insecurity.

Legs and Feet Will Normally Point

In the Direction of Interest.

What the Legs and Feet Are Saying

UNCROSSED LEGS – Shows openness.

CROSSED WHEN SITTING – Indicates caution disinterest.

OPEN WHEN SITTING – Shows arrogance or is combative.

ANKLE LOCKED SITTING – Is defensive

PARALELL CLOSE TOGETHER WHEN SITTING – Shows a Proper position.

When Standing

STANDING LEGS WIDE APART – Aggressive ready for action

STANDING AT ATTENTION – Is Respectful

STANDING LEGS CROSSED – Shows insecurity or submission.

STANDING KNEES BUCKLING – Under pressure

FOOT FORWARD STANDING – Directed toward a dominant group Member

3. Body Positioning

1. The Confident Stance

Hands clasped in front – at hip level

Feet are slightly more than hip width apart.

Chest is slightly raised.

This is the best way to start your presentation as it immediately portrays confidence and assumes the authoritative position

It creates a very positive appearance and a person who is knowledgeable. You are now in **Control.**

2. The Jester Request for Answer Stance

Open out your hands just above waist height, on each side

The wider they are apart; the more emphatic is the message

Palms up

Eyebrows raised

Head turned slightly

For a yes or no question

It is used often when one wishes to emphasize the need for an answer or are asking the audience to simply think for themselves.

This position can be subtle or can be greatly exaggerated depending on the situation.

The exaggeration of it, can also inject humor into your speech or presentation and ease tension or regain attention.

3. The Leveler – Authority

Stand Erect

Put arms with palms down in front of you

Fingers open

Move hands and finger tips up and down in a fanning motion

If the audience is getting restless or noisy or are applauding or laughing at something you have said or done, this is a good way to assume control again in a polite but authoritative way.

Usually no words are necessary to achieve the results you want, and it is all done with the effective use of body language.

4. The Thinker

Raise one hand to your face

Thumb under chin

Index finger on one side of your nose

Other fingers folded resting on chin other side of nose

Other hand under elbow of think arm

Elbows at mid chest range

PAUSE briefly with hands in this position. Remove the hand and deliver your message with authority

This can be used subtly to indicate you really are thinking. It is often used when someone has asked you a question. You can pause to think about the question.

It can be exaggerated in a humorous way. Many comedians will use this stance to obtain laughs without even speaking a word. Once you use it for humor it will probably lose the effect of your serious think-mode, if you try to go back.

5. The Joker

One hand on hip

Other arm raised in air about head level, stretched out, with Palm up

Leaning slightly back

Stomach out

Smiling or laughing

This can really project humor and can generate a lot of fun into your presentation at the appropriate time. It can be used to express an outrageous response for humor.

It can be used simply as a spontaneous reaction or you can "of course" stage it which is the most common use.

6. Questions – Show of Hands Everyone

For audiences of 5 plus

You Ask – *"Are there any questions"?*

Raise one hand high above your head palm out

Other hand down at side

Stand on toes

Wait for audience hands to rise

With your raised arm, point to the person who will ask the question. Then put your arm down

Repeat until no more questions

At the end of your presentation when you ask for question it is often hard to get this Q & A part going.

This gesture will usually do the trick and get the ball rolling. Get into the habit of using this as it is an easy way to get a response.

4. Personal Space

Personal space requirements will depend on personality and culture and environmental conditioning and the relationship with the other person(s) involved.

Edward T Hall in 1914

Originally identified the five distinct space zones and that interpretation remains the same to present day.

Hall's study interprets the amount of space that people find comfortable between themselves and others as it relates to their social intimacy with that person.

The term asking for one's space is representative of asking for respect in what is comfortable for a person.

When someone moves within these boundaries they are said to be invading or violating one's personal space.

Such a move will often cause the person being intruded upon to step back or feel challenged, pressured or overpowered. This maneuver is often used to take control of a situation.

THE FIVE ZONES of Personal Space

Zone one - 0 to 6 inches - CLOSE INTIMATE – Physical contact intimacy

Zone two - 6 to 18 inches - INTIMATE – Close friends, sports

Zone three - 18 inches to 48 inches PERSONAL – Family and close friends

Zone four - 4 feet to 12 feet - SOCIAL – Consultative

Zone five - Over 12 feet - PUBLIC – No interaction

Summary to Communication

Once a person has mastered Communication, they have already set the agenda for Success in Selling.

Communication creates the framework for our sales efforts. Becoming a good or great communicator allows the sales person to deliver a focused, clear message to their prospect.

All our Skills Involve Communication

Having a successful meeting or sales presentation depends on how well one can deliver their message.

PRESENTATIONS

The Basics

There are different styles of presentations or meetings depending on the size of the order or the reason for the meeting. It is important to know the differences and how to prepare for each type to obtain optimum results.

Types of Meetings

1. Introductory – First Meetings
2. Fact Finding – additional Meetings
3. Dress Rehearsal
4. Final Presentations
5. The Call Back

We will outline all the above types of meetings separately, as each will have its own purpose and structure.

Delivering a Presentation

Starting the Presentation

1. Open with a very short story or a great comment can be good.
2. Do not overdo the short story.
3. Make sure the comment is relevant and in good taste.
4. Maybe use a bit of Humor.
    - It loosens up an audience and enhances memory.
5. Too much humor can make it difficult to get serious again.

Throughout the Presentation

- Use Body Language and voice tones for affect.
- Be descriptive and paint a picture with your words.
- Use quotes from famous people, only if they fit the situation
- Often quotes will create Interest; but, make sure you know them and can deliver them accurately.
- Use statistics to add impact.

- Use power words.
- Share something to create emotion and involve them.
- Use opinions from experts.

Closing the Presentation

1. Have a Summary – Your call to Action
2. Promise Hope for the future.
3. End on a positive note.
4. Do not introduce new information after you have finished unless you are asked.

Presentation Things to Do

Do – Know your material.

Do – Tell it and do not read it

Do – Focus on your message.

Do – Show that you believe in what you are saying.

Do – Focus on their needs.

Do – Have a structure that they can follow.

Do – Talk with enthusiasm

Do - Demonstrate confidence in your voice tones

Do – Make eye contact with audience. Hold for count of 3 elephants for maximum effect.

Do – Use gestures that enhance your message. (body language)

Do – Dress up not down. They need to look up to you as authority.

Do – USE THE 3 T's

1. Tell them what you are going to tell them.
2. Tell them.
3. Tell them what you have just told them.

Do – Use the 3 P's – Practice, Practice, and Practice.

Do – Use the 10:20:30 rule

- 10 slides
- 20 minutes
- 30 font size

Presentation Mistakes

- There are many mistakes made when people make presentations. We have outlined a few most common ones that occur.
- Spelling errors – Break concentration and destroy credibility.
- Little or no preparation – You look disorganized or confused and unprofessional.
- Practice is a must! - You will look organized knowledgeable and professional.

Lack of Structure

Often people do not follow a logical sequence when creating their presentation.

If it is not organized, it becomes difficult to follow.

1. If your message is not clear and is not focused
   - The prospect becomes confused and loses interest.
2. If there is too much information
   - You wear out your welcome.

Messaging

- The Filler Words - Get rid of them! – The use of (Uum's, so's aaw's, and's) – will make your presentation weak and boring.
- If your Presentation is ME focused not CLIENT focused. - It is annoying to them.
- Remember their needs *WIIFM, - "What's in It for Me."*
- It's what THEY want. - This is not about you!
- Wrong mission statement – No one cares about your mission statement. It's their goals they want to reach.
- Your ideas appear too radical or they do not solve the client's problems or meet their needs.

Afraid to Engage

Often people will avoid a Q & A period because they cannot rehearse. This will usually occur if they do not know their material well enough.

If one does this, the audience will feel left out

They may even be Angry

Mistakes with Support Materials

Visuals

- Too many slides or brochures
- Not enough or none
- Find the right balance

Reading information on slides or brochures to your audience is a *"Big Mistake"*

You can speak at 100 words per minute and your audience can read at 200 words per minute. - This can totally disrupt a presentation.

If you are going to use information on slides, keep it point form. People will not read long paragraphs of material on slides.

If using brochures, do not provide too many or clients will lose focus and interest.

Mistakes Using Point Form.

- Too Much of one type of power point will lose its effectiveness
- Size is too small
- Too bright or too dull
- Bad color choice – Find out the best Colors to use for the purpose.

All the above mistakes are Irritating to the prospect and will cause them to disengage.

Delivery Mistakes

- Weak Openings – There is no attention getter.
- Weak Closings – There is no strong "Call to Action".
- Meeting is too long – Keep under 25 minutes or have breaks.
- Too Much of a Monotone

Remember Voice/Enthusiasm

No indication when you are changing topics. - You lose their attention.

Too much movement – Upsets or irritates your audience.

Too little movement – It is boring and does not inspire.

Presentations - Not to Do

Do not - Be afraid of silence- It is often more powerful than noise

Do not – Have too much continuous content in your presentation.

Do not have long sessions over 25 minutes. Separate it and take short breathers. 17.5 minutes is the average attention span.

Do not – Abuse slides - Too fast, too slow and Especially not knowing what they are!

Do not – Make the presentation one-way traffic only – Engage the client.

Do not - Dwell on your company history etc.

Do not - Boast about your company profits! They will think that they are next to be added to your list.

You May Laugh – But I have seen it Happen

Side Conversations

Often you may find that people in your audience will start having their own little discussions and this can be very disruptive.

Do not be rude or Ask them to Stop Talking

If you are interrupted by others having a conversation while you are speaking:

You can say:

"I see there may be a question. Can I help you with it?"

"I sense there is a question over here. Can I help you with it?"

Lastly - Do Not EVER!

- Try and bluff your way through an answer.
- If you do not have the answer just say that's a great question and I will get back to you on that.
- If you try to bluff it, you could discredit your entire presentation by providing the wrong information. **GET BACK TO THEM!**

THE FIRST MEETING

Overview

Be Prepared

The very first meeting will provide your greatest opportunity to make the right first impression and to start building your relationship.

The Prospect's respect and trust of your company and its offerings; will start, with the first impression that you will make.

You are there to create interest, find out if there are needs and gather the information that you will require for your quotation.

Dangerous

The greatest danger is to underestimate the importance of this part of the sales process. Some people will not prepare themselves properly.

They just make the appointment and show up for the meeting with no agenda.

They "Wing it" as the Saying goes

There Could Be Nothing Worse

It is here that you will bring together all the good things and benefits of your company, its products and services, and present them to an important decision maker.

It is here that your prospect will be the most receptive to hear what you should say.

If you do a Good Job

They will provide you with an opportunity to quote your products or services. If it is done properly; it will also make it possible for you to obtain a purchase order, to supply their needs.

You are there to gather information on how you can help this customer. It represents the beginning of finding out what their needs are. It will enable you to offer the right products, services or solutions.

It is also the opportunity to overcome negative thoughts, or incorrect information, that the customer may have obtained about your company, its products or services. *(Often provided by competition)*

What You Need

Start with the suggestions that we are providing in these chapters and establish the initial outline for your introductory meetings.

It will take three or four first meetings with new prospects to adjust and create an acceptable outline that you will eventually follow for all first meetings.

Once Created

Do not Stop There – Build on It

Constantly strive for improvement and use your experience to expand and make the content and delivery better.

Once you have created this blueprint for first meetings you will be able to make the minor adjustments to suit each new prospect.

If you continue to strive for improvement of your content and delivery, your closing percentages will get better as well.

Prospect Knowledge

You are there to learn how you can help the prospect. You do this by discovering their needs and finding solutions to their problem areas.

- Research the company you are visiting before you go so that you are familiar with:
    - Its management team,
    - Their products,
    - Size of facilities, Number of employees etc.
- Check them out with your peers and on the internet and find out all the information that you can.
- You want to be able to speak with confidence and authority and can demonstrate that you have done your homework and are there to help them wherever possible.

Questions for Preparing your Agenda Outline

- Whom do you wish to see?
- What will be your opening statements?

- What questions will you ask?
- What do you want to achieve?
- What will be your Closing Statement?
- What will be your Summary - *"Call to Action?"*

Support Materials

- What support Information about your company will you need?
- What Information about your offerings will you need?
- What references or testimonials will you use?

Tips for the First Meeting

- Arrive on time and make sure your appearance is professional.
- Speak clearly, not too quickly and pause occasionally.
- Be Polite, Show Respect. Ask permission to use first names.
- Show Interest in what they are saying.
- Listen to their answers
- Write the answers down to any of your questions.
    - Do not try to remember the answers to write them down later.
    - You will usually forget something, and it could be a key item.
    - Writing the answers down also shows respect and that you are thorough in your job.

Ask if there are any questions or areas of concern about your company or offerings when you are done.

Most of all - Thank them for their Time and Attention

And for any Opportunity Given

The customer is always right until they find out; on their own, that they are wrong.

- NEVER tell them or imply they are wrong.
- You are there to prove them right by listening to you.

An Introductory Presentation

All first-time meetings with a customer will involve the same concept. They will be your introductory meeting where you present your company and its offerings.

It will also be where you will find out the true extent of the prospects needs and their desire to consider your offerings.

The Types of First Meeting Will Vary

1. Some will be for smaller products, offerings or volumes
2. Some may be larger orders for annual supply requiring secondary visits.
3. Some may be process equipment or projects that will require many additional visits to gather all the facts and specifications.

The need to prepare for this initial meeting will be equally important for small or large. The questions asked, and number of people involved will differ. The Preparation and final presentations will also change.

Requirements for Your Meeting

a) Initial Qualifying – Before arranging the meeting make sure the reason for it is clear to the prospect.

b) Agenda - Although optional, it is always best to have one.

c) Introduction - Introducing your company and your products or services. State the purpose of the meeting when you start.

Your Company Information

1. Have a brief written history of 1 or 2 pages showing your present management, special skills, testimonials or awards.
2. Have brochures or information on your products or services
3. Do not hand this information out at this point. If you do they will start reading and you will lose their attention.
4. Deliver a verbal point-form summary of 1 & 2
5. Before you leave, hand out your information and brochures

They now have a Reminder

Of your Visit

d) Their Company Information

- **Needs** – Before you begin any in depth promotional efforts of your offerings, confirm their specific interests or needs.
- **Interest** – Confirm they will consider changing suppliers?

e) Product description - Clearly describe your product in terms your client will understand. Speak their language not yours. Tell your audience what you have for them.

- **Benefits** - Outline the normal product or service benefits as they relate to the client's needs. Give examples of where you feel that you can help them.
- **Successes** - To drive home a point, mention some of your successes and have names and/or written testimonials available to show the client.

f) Positioning - Mention your unique projects.

- Show why you are better or different from your competitors.
- Show how you have solved difficult customer requirements where others could not.

g) Closing Comments – Your comments here will set the stage for your final part on your agenda. - It is the introduction to your "- Call to Action"

h) Summary - *"Call to Action"* – Based on the reasons for your meeting, you will be asking for:

- A Request to Quote
- Further Action to be taken
- A Request for a Purchase Order.

NOTE: Never ever refer to this part on your agenda when showing it or speaking to the prospect as a **"Call-to-Action."** It is a **"Summary"**

i) Undertakings - Establish what they will be doing and what you will be doing for the next meeting.

Use this as your basic requirements for your first meeting. Most first meetings will have a common purpose and that is to introduce your company and establish needs.

What will vary will be the opportunity types, which we will discuss in the next chapters.

The Two Main Opportunity Types

Type One will be for normal day to day needs of your products or services. They may be purchased weekly, monthly or as annual blanket contracts for supplies or services

These Types of Opportunities Could Involve:

- A one-time meeting for very simple and straight forward purchases. Sometimes no repeat orders are involved.
- Several meetings for introduction, sampling and quoting of the customer's needs for daily, monthly or annual requirements
- It could involve several meetings to solve a problem

Type Two will be for special onetime purchases involving:

Larger pieces of office equipment or plant equipment

Large Systems or Projects

These meetings will usually involve many additional fact-finding meetings and many people on both sides.

There are usually different specifications and customer requirements that need to be met.

Type 1 - Day-to-Day Needs

The Purpose for the Meeting

1) It could be a single visit for a one-time sale.

2) You could be gathering information to quote on some of their weekly production consumables, production services, office supplies or shipping supplies or services.

3) You may be gathering information and providing samples for annual consumption of materials or for annual service contracts.

Examples

It could be their packaging materials, chemicals, paint, photocopy supplies, or any part of their daily, weekly or monthly needs.

Usually these types of orders are usually handled by:

- The Purchasing Department,
- Plant, Production or Office Manages
- Maintenance or Shipping Departments
- Or a combination of them.

Usually upper management is not involved in smaller daily, weekly or monthly ordering requirements.

For larger purchases such as their monthly supply of steel, paint or components for their manufacturing process, you will usually become involved with quality control and/or engineering in addition to the above.

Sample Questions you might Ask

- What do they know about your company and offerings?
- Do they know anyone who is using your products or services?
- What have they heard from these people?
- What is important for them in a supplier?
- Are they happy with their present supplier's?
    - Deliveries?
    - Service?

  - Price?
  - Quality?
- Are they looking for improvement anywhere?
- Do they have any problem areas that need solving?
- Who is supplying their needs presently?
- Ask if you could provide them with samples or a quotation for comparison?
    - Ask for quantities, specifications or technical data if required.
- Ask to see their operation "if possible".
- Ask for their business card and email address?
- Ask who else is involved in the decision making?

Allow space to write in answers and any undertakings.

Distribution of copies

Ask how many will attend the decision-making meetings and always make extra copies.

The 30 Minute Timeline

It is important that you have set your agenda to suit the time allowed for your first meeting.

The time we are suggesting for this type of customer needs is approximately 30 minutes in length.

It will be up to the prospect to choose if that time line is extended. If they do it is a good sign.

The Sample Timeline

Introduction and General Description -	3 to 4 minutes
General questions including authority -	1 to 2 minutes
Specific prepared questions -	14 to 15 minutes
Summary - (Call to Action)	4 to 6 minutes
Undertakings - Set time line to establish	2 to 3 minutes
Total time -	**24 to 30 minutes**

Note: If your outline is completed within the above time frame you will have shown respect for their time and demonstrated your organizational skills.

Summary (Call to Action)

Most of the time this is an introductory and information gathering meeting and you will do a quick summary of the main points.

Occasionally it might be a presentation for an item that needs no research or additional visit.

Here your call to action will be to ask for the Order.

Undertakings

If additional information is required, it is proper to ask if the prospect has any additional time available to gather it while you are there or ask if you should come back.

This is also where you will establish the things to do for you next meeting.

If there is further action to be provided by the prospect this will also be part of the Undertakings.

Set the time line for completion of any undertakings to take place.

Make it as quickly as possible, so that the momentum is not lost, and your first meeting does not become a distant memory to either party.

Undertakings Follow-up

After your first meeting follow up by email when you are back in the office and thank them for their time and the opportunity.

There will usually be some undertakings that your client will have and some that you will have.

Provide a Short Outline of:

- What they will be doing
- What you will be doing
- Show the time frame that is involved
- Send it to them.

The easier you make this part the better they will like it and they will be more likely to do it quickly.

Summary of Type 1 First Meeting

Once you have created and perfected your first one-on-one meeting or presentation, you have overcome one of the greatest failures of many people in sales.

How to Successfully Organize and Hold
A First Introductory Meeting

Experience demonstrates the necessity to be organised and deliver a great first meeting. Unfortunately, many will not see the significance.

Importance of Practice

Once you have put your first meeting presentation together, it is time to practice your delivery of it. Nothing is worse than going unprepared and looking like it.

You have done all this work to get ready so rehearse by delivering it to someone at your office, a family member or in front of a mirror or all.

Get feedback on the way it comes across. Ask for suggestions for improvement. Once you have made any adjustments, it is time to practice, practice, and practice some more until you can deliver it with perfection.

Your first meetings will be very important not only to impress your client, but to observe how your client reacts to your information.

You do not want to have to worry about remembering what to say and not be able to observe the reactions and amount of interest shown by your prospect.

Confidence Builder

Having this area perfected as a skill set; will give you control and confidence, when you are making your first appointments.

Type 2 - Larger Equipment and Projects

General Project Meeting

Reason for this General Project Meeting

Our starting point here is that you initially made contact and talked with the prospect's project manager by phone or in a meeting like the one just outlined. This is the result of that discussion.

This is your first General Meeting with the main people who are involved in the project.

People from your company and your prospect's company will now take part so that everyone involved can become familiar with each other.

Basic Preparation for your Meeting

You should have previously established how many will attend this meeting for distribution of your introductory information. Always make extra copies

Introductions at Meeting

1. Introduce yourself, your company and anyone else attending with you.
2. Ask for a quick introduction of those attending the meeting from the prospects side. This is often a good time to exchange cards if it has not already been done.

3. Provide a brief verbal outline of your company's offerings, its history and accomplishments, (You will hand out your written copy at the end).

You might Ask

- What they know of your company, products or equipment?
- Do they know of anyone who has your systems or equipment?
- What have they heard about these installations?

Be Prepared

This is where you will be called upon for the types of knowledge that we have discussed earlier.

The main purpose for you is to present the best picture of your company possible. It will be your first impression and perhaps determine if you will proceed further.

The Next Move is Really Theirs

For them it could simply have been a meeting to assess you and your company's capabilities of handling an order or project of this size and they will be the ones who are asking most of the questions.

They will be Controlling the Time and Direction

If You Qualify

If they feel you meet their initial requirements, they may immediately begin by getting more specific and allow more detailed questions.

So Be Prepared to Continue!

Our Model for Discussion

"A Plant Processing System". will be the example project that we will use for outlining things that need to be done and the questions we will ask.

The actual questions for different types of large orders or projects will vary depending on your company's offerings and the size of the potential order.

If you can ask these types of questions during this first meeting, that is a very positive sign.

You should be prepared to undertake this part even if you think that the prospect may not be ready to get into the specifics during this meeting with them.

Types of Questions that you will ask.

These questions could be asked (all or in part) at any time that is suitable during this meeting or your future project kick-off meeting.

Much of the following information could be covered by the prospect and you may not use some or most of these sample questions. We are providing them as examples of what you should know.

About the Project

- What are the reasons for their new project?
- Do they have a project description or list of specifications?
- Who will be your main contact to gather information and present your final proposal to.
- What are their production requirements?

- What parts of the project do they want to handle – if any?
    - Do they want?
        - Turn-key?
        - Equipment only?
        - Install only?
- What is the time frame for delivery?
- When is the full quotation required by?
- Who else is quoting? (*they may not provide this*)
- When will they be selecting the supplier (placing the order)?

Find out the names of everyone that you will be working with on the project. Ask for their business cards and email addresses.

Get the names of anyone else who will be getting copies of your recommendations.

Final Questions

- Ask them how many copies of information or drawings they will normally require for presentations.
- What plant area have they set aside for the equipment and ask if it is possible to view the area while you are there?
- Find out what their safety requirements are for visiting the plant or manufacturing area. Make sure you always have safety shoes, safety glasses and a hard hat with you.

Summary – *"Your Call to action"*

This is where you will establish your undertakings for you next meeting. If there is further action to be provided by the prospect this will also be part of the call to action.

Set the time line for completion of any undertakings to take place as quickly as possible so that you do not lose any momentum and your first meeting does not become a distant memory to either party.

Undertakings

After your first meeting follow up by email when you are back in the office and thank them for their time and the opportunity.

There will usually be some undertakings that your client will have and some that you will have.

Provide a short outline of:

- What they will be doing and what you will be doing
- Show the time frame that is involved
- Send it to them.

The easier you make this part the better they will like it and they will be more likely to do it quickly.

Summary of General Project Meeting

We have provided an example of a typical project meeting. It is meant as a general overview of what you can expect for meetings of this nature.

One of the main things to remember, is to make sure you have more than enough copies of information foe everyone in attendance.

The person who goes without might play a key role at some point in the project. Do not alienate them at the starting line.

This meeting timeline will normally be set and organized by your prospect. Because of this you will not have presented an agenda of your own.

Other than your introductions and questions outlined it will be almost an open forum and agenda.

Exception to a First One-on-One Meeting

Project Presentation to all Competition as a Group

You may have been invited because of your Company Branding and Marketing, or from your initial contact and first meeting.

Very often a company will invite all the people who will be bidding on a large order or project to a general Kick-Off meeting. Here the agenda will again be set by the prospect and here you will largely become a spectator.

Usually you will introduce yourself and your company representatives, at some point. The other people who are bidding will do the same.

If this happens, make sure you write down all the company names, so you will know who you are up against.

The prospect will usually provide a general outline of the project, when and where it will take place. There may be some general specifications, but this is more of an invitation to bid.

After this meeting you will have your one-on-one kick-off meeting. It will probably be as an additional fact-finding session, which will be very much like the first meeting we just described.

Project Kick-Off after Group Meeting

Reason for Meeting

This is the first One-on-One Project kick off meeting that will follow the Group style we just discussed.

The first presentation of your company was at the group meeting and very little opportunity was given to promote it. You are now there for the one-on-one kick off meeting for the project.

The general parameters were set at the group meeting, but you are here for more specific information regarding the project. It is the beginning of a more personal relationship with those involved in the project.

A similar list will be prepared to request the information that you still need to continue the preparation of your offerings.

It is important that you have set your agenda to suit the time allowed for your first one-on-one meeting.

The time we are suggesting is approximately 45 - 60 minutes in length. It will be up to the prospect to choose if that time line is extended. If they do it is a good sign.

The 45 - 60 Minute Time Line

Introductions	1 – 2 Minutes
Presentation of your Company -	6 to 8 minutes
Discussion of Project	15 to 20 minutes
Specific prepared questions -	14 to 15 minutes
Summary - (Your call to Action)	7 to 12 minutes
Undertakings - Set time line to establish	2 to 3 minutes
Total time -	**45 to 60 minutes**

If additional information is required; it is proper to ask if the prospect has any time available to gather it while you are there, or shall you come back.

Summary

Once you have created and perfected your first outline for this type of meeting, you have accomplished another blueprint for success.

Experience does teach the necessity to be organised and deliver a great first meeting. Do not delay. Get this important part of your selling tool kit ready for use.

Importance of Practice (Restated to Emphasize)

- Once you have put your first meeting presentation together, it is time to practice your delivery of it.
- Nothing is worse than going unprepared and looking like it.
- You have done all this work to get ready so rehearse by delivering it to someone at your office, a family member or in front of a mirror or all.
- Get feedback on the way it comes across. Ask for suggestions for improvement.
- Once you have made the adjustments, it is time to practice, practice, and practice some more until you can deliver it with perfection.
- Your first meetings will be very important not only to impress your client, but to observe how your client reacts to your information.
- You do not want to have to worry about remembering what to say and not be able to observe the reactions and amount of interest shown by your prospect.

Confidence Builder

Having this area perfected as a skill set will give you control and confidence when you are making your appointments.

FACT FINDING MEETINGS

1) Type 1 - Weekly, Monthly, Annual Needs

Reason for this Type

Sometimes there may be a second or even a third meeting to obtain additional information, depending on the size of order or technical information in question.

These meetings are usually quicker than the initial meeting and less structured. There may also be some sampling and testing before you arrive at your recommendations and prices.

Have a plan. Be totally organized and know what you wish to accomplish at or during these meeting. Have an agenda to hand out with your questions and list of things that you need to know.

The same fact-finding process will exist for services that are multi-faceted and may involve several departments and a few visits.

Benefits of Additional Meetings

Having several meetings before you make your formal presentation should be considered as "very beneficial" in the sales process.

The client will get to know both you and your company better during these subsequent meetings. You can also monitor your progress.

When this Occurs

You will no longer be a stranger and if you have presented yourself well and listened well, you are doing what it takes to build TRUST.

Always remember to follow the same protocol as outlined earlier and remember to thank them each time for seeing you. Once you have all the information you need from the client, you are ready to start putting your main presentation or quotation together for products and services.

2) Type 2 - Large Equipment or Projects

Reason for this Type

For large projects for systems or equipment, there are usually several subsequent meetings where you are gathering all the required information.

These are also less structured and usually quicker in and out type meetings. You may also be taking measurements in the plant or speaking to other plant employees involved as well.

There will often be group meetings with more people depending on the size or complexity of the project. These will be longer meetings. The same parameters apply. Have a plan and agenda outlining your objectives and things you need to know.

Benefits (restated)

Having a few meetings before you make your formal presentation should be considered beneficial as the client and others involved will get to know both you and your company better.

You will no longer be a stranger and if you have presented yourself well and listened well, you are again doing what it takes to build TRUST.

In each of these subsequent meetings, always remember to follow the same protocol as outlined earlier and thank them each time for seeing you.

Also use these meetings to monitor your progress.

If you can take pictures of the area to be occupied, as they could possibly be used in your presentation.

Once you have all the information you need from the client, you are ready to start putting your main presentation or quotation together.

SALES PRESENTATIONS

General Guidelines

You have gathered all the information required and you will now be preparing the document for your presentation. We will outline your preparation for four types of sales presentation meetings.

Meeting Types

1. The 35 Minute meeting
2. The 60 Minute Dress Rehearsal
3. The Final Presentation
4. The Call Back

It is important to structure your presentations to enable you to make trial closes throughout your delivery. This will allow you to make sure you are on track.

Getting this confirmation in small steps is much more effective than waiting for the completion of your final presentation to see where you stand.

If they are in the habit of saying yes to the small closes, the order will come much easier at the end.

Discovery of Opposition

You also will get negative responses to some of your trial closes. It will be important to be able to uncover the reasons for their reactions and change them to a positive situation.

Knowing how to close and overcome objections is essential.

We mention using these two areas closing and overcoming objections because they are part of the reasoning behind how you will construct your presentations.

Your goal is to have the prospect on your side when you get to the final closing question and your presentation is how you get there.

We are outlining the ways to put your presentations together to be able to reach a positive outcome at the end.

There will be a big difference between the quoting of everyday requirements and major equipment or projects. These differences will be reflected in the size of quotations (number of pages) and the time it takes to deliver them.

Some Things You Must Do

- Identify and eliminate any of your own internal company jargon.
- Use specific words and phrases that your audience uses and understands.
- Simplify any of your complex technical terms and subject matter.
- Be prepared with short answers to questions that might occur.

During your presentation, you should move forward by building on your last point. Do not just begin a new area or topic without any warning.

Construct your presentation in a logical sequence that is easy to follow. Do not jump from topic to topic in a random order or you will surely lose their interest and comprehension.

People must understand and relate to what you have said, what you are saying and what you are about to say to fully grasp your message.

If there is any point in your presentation where people can become even slightly confused, you are at high risk of disconnecting with your entire audience.

You Must

- Follow a logical sequence.
- Items out of sequence will lose your audience.
- **Notify** your audience when you are about to switch to different subject matter.
- **Use:**
    - Audience Participation
    - Examples of Success
    - Stories, or Magic Moments, the "WOW" factor
    - Visuals and Props

The Presentation Basics

1. Establish the Framework first – the Story outline.
2. Carefully plan your Opening minute to grab their attention.
3. Outline your Main thoughts.
4. Spice it up. - Sometimes a picture is worth 1000 words.

If your quotation is only 3 to 5 pages and there is no support material, then it makes more sense to hand them the document and give them time to read it.

- Do not read the 3 to 5 pages to them.
- Have a point form document for discussion once they are done reading the proposal.
- Then discuss your solutions and benefits point by point

For 6 – 12+ pages of information delivered to small groups, the use of your lap top or other mobile device can act as a great presentation delivery system.

- Use a summary-point-form delivery format
- Hand out the full hard copy document at the end.

For larger groups the use of a slide projection system and larger screen is very effective.

- Use a summary point form delivery format in your slides
- Again, tell it - do not read it.
- Hand out the full written document at the end.

General Notes

- All quotations should contain a point form section that covers the key features and benefits of your offerings.
- For smaller quotations, it could be one page or less.
- For larger presentations, it could be two or three.
- You will use this as a base outline in your presentation.

It is best to avoid providing too much written detail before you make your entire presentation as people naturally want to read on their own. Many will immediately search for the price page.

We Suggest the Following Procedure

The following format should best control the meeting. In this way, you will avoid everyone reading your entire quotation at their own pace. If you allow this to happen, you will lose control of the meeting.

Explain what you are doing before you start.

a) Have Three Sections

1) Your Features Page(s)
2) Your Pricing Page(s)
3) Your Full Detailed Quotation

1) First - Your Features Page.

- Hand out and make sure it is in point form
- Memorize its sequence; but, deliver a longer version verbally.
- Explain that this is a summary of everything they have asked for or require
- Do not just read the point form. Refer to it but use your own expanded explanation of the point form
- Explain you will hand out the detailed version when you are done and the reason for your method is for clarity.

Delivered the right way, your message will be condensed and clear and will be remembered more easily.

- They will use the point form to follow your progress
- They will retain it for a reference after the meeting

You Do Not want your Message to be Encumbered

With a lot of Descriptive Fluff

Where the Message can be Easily Lost

The Features part is made up of key points to explain and maintain attention.

These points will be based on the following

- You asked for this and we gave you this
- You needed this and that is what we gave you.
- You must be able to deliver this without reading it.

Writing your points on a white board works well. Keep it short!

Using a pointer where your points are on a screen is good. (again, very shortened points)

The Detailed part is Usually Saved for Later Discussions

The last thing that you want for your presentation is for all to open the detailed document and sit silently as each person reads at their own pace.

Personal experience has shown this will be a disaster

If you attempt to read it out loud to them, they are finished reading the page by the time you are only half done your verbal presentation.

You are on page 2 and they are on 4

If you continue reading, it is soon realized that everyone has become disconnected, you lose complete control and you will have very little chance of achieving your goal, call to action or getting an order.

You Must

Memorize it.

Practice it until it has reached perfection and you can cover the key points quickly.

During the first minute the audience is deciding if it is worth their time to listen. It may be your only chance to create their real desire to listen or if they will half-listen or just pretend that they are listening.

If their Eyes Are Glazed or Blank

You are in Trouble

2) Next - Pricing and Terms and Conditions Page(s)

Hand out and show the base price

If there are options show them as add on prices separately.

If you have an ROI (Return on Investment) show it here.

If there is a financing option show it here

For a longer terms and conditions remember to make it a feature and brag about it. Let them read it and then discuss it.

3) Last - Detailed Description Section

Hand out your support documents

- Pictures
- References or Testimonials

Give them a minute to absorb the package and ask if they wish to review it in detail now.

By handling everything this way; management can stay long enough to hear your quick outline and the price, and then leave if they wish.

They will leave the details for others to review unless they are a hands-on type person.

If they stay for the Detailed Section

You know they are Interested.

Why Memorize?

One often spends most of their time putting the content together and little attention is paid to how it will be delivered. Practice and test your presentation because the prospects like it when you are well prepared.

A practiced and polished delivery will make a big difference in your closing capability. It also provides the confidence to make a great presentation and can observe their reaction to it.

To Take Them on an Emotional Journey

You Must Be Totally Prepared!

If you have not practiced and perfected the delivery of your presentation before you arrive, it will not be effective, and you will not build their confidence or trust.

Clarity is the Foundation for Persuasion

35 MINUTE FINAL PRESENTATION

Overview

In the 35-minute presentation you are usually providing a simple 2 to 7-page quotation for smaller items that do not have a lot of information attached to them. You may be presenting it to only one to three people.

The total meeting time will be scheduled to take a maximum of 35 minutes in length including questions pricing and call to action (request for order).

Four Tips

1. The best way to ensure success is to cover the key points in your main presentation in 15 - 17 minutes.
2. It is said that the average uninterrupted attention span in a meeting is 17.5 minutes.
3. If the main delivery part of a meeting is 25 minutes or over, it can easily get out of control and become boring and monotonous, and finish on a negative note.
4. Have a mini break of 1 – 2 minutes' midpoint if it is much over 20 minutes.

How to Organize

When you have found out who will need personalized copies, prepare enough copies for everyone and have some extras. In most cases these meetings will be small in the number of people present.

You Must

- Have an agenda that includes your time-line allowed
- Prepare and provide a brief history of yourself and your company to deliver verbally and a hard copy to hand out.

The Main Delivery

- Provide a summarized copy of your presentation in point form hand it out; but, deliver it from memory

The Outline: (Point Form)

- The purpose of your presentation (their requirements)
- Your recommendations to meet their needs (your offerings)
- The benefits, solutions they get by using your offerings

Pricing

- Provide your prices and their optional extras later after your key points. Keep it as a separate section.

Detailed Section (Support Materials)

For the detailed section, (which you will hand out at the end).

- Include support information that will show how your product/services will help your prospect to resolve any existing problems or concerns that you uncovered in your initial questions.

Use your Sales Aids

Use slides and power point, product data and technical information, testimonials and samples.

Detailed Information

Have very specific technical data only, for the main presentation.

- Avoid too much detail in your presentation. Keep it simple.
- You will usually hand out the additional detailed technical information separately at the end, or when required for discussion

Extra Copies

Make extras for them to hand out to others of their own choice. Do not guess at who gets them or who does not. Let them decide.

Questions

After the main presentation, open the meeting for a short discussion and questions.

Be prepared to answer questions

Close the Sale

1. Have your objectives or call to action clearly defined.
2. Have a well-rehearsed transition from your presentation to the Q&A and then to your call to action.
3. If the meeting is for the order - Have your closes ready.
4. Be prepared to answer any objections that may arise which should be considered reasons to buy.

Sample Meeting Time Line

Introduction –	1 to 3 minutes
Main Delivery	15 to16 minutes
Have a Q&A session.	5 to 6 minutes
Discuss Pricing	3 to 4 minutes
Final Q & A	1 to 3 minutes
Summary (Call to action)	2 to 3 minutes
Total –	**27 to 35 minutes**

Optional

A longer Q&A or pricing discussion should be by the client's choice. Hand out the pricing information to management and let them decide who stays or gets a copy.

Other Items to consider

- The 17.5-minute attention span does not include introductions or handing out information but refers to the verbal delivery part of the main content of your message.
- It is best to arrive ahead of time to set up any equipment needed for your presentation.
- You keep your start time on time.
- Delays come from others not you.
- If more senior key personnel are present (which can be the case) along with your contact, it is polite to let them know your agenda and time line to cover the information.
- Provide them with a copy of everything. Explain how you handle pricing.
- Ask if they might need to get away so you can cover the important areas for them first
- It's a great excuse to speak with the senior decision makers.

Make your Agenda Time Line Scalable.

Show the times you have allowed for each part of your agenda. Now the prospect is aware of what will take palace and how long you have allowed for it.

If they decide to extend any part of the agenda, they will also realize what happens to the time line.

Tell them your plan and give them the option to expand any area that the feel needs more time to cover.

If you know they have allowed more time for your presentation in advance, make your adjustments and show the new times on your agenda to suit the new total time allowed.

60 MINUTE DRESS REHEARSAL

The Overview

Why Have a Dress Rehearsal?

We call it our dress rehearsal.

To the Customer it will be a **Final Review Meeting** to make sure you have all the facts right and no new things have changed the scope of the requirements or project details.

This type of meeting is for the larger offering packages, equipment or projects. This meeting should be considered essential by you as your dress rehearsal before any final presentation is made.

It is also your Trial Close

The Request

Insist on having this Final Review Meeting. It is your review platform to see if you have correctly assessed all their needs and have all the solutions they require.

It is also a chance to see where you are positioned before final recommendations and final prices are provided.

Your Own Reason for the Final Review Meeting

Your company has perhaps spent 150 to 250 hours or more of their time so far; for questions, research, and design, engineering and proposal and pricing assembly.

It should be normal procedure required by your company or you to see if the final presentation will be accurate and complete.

The Dress Rehearsal Benefits

The reason for this dress rehearsal is the same as a dress rehearsal for any play. It is to find out where your weak points are before you make your debut (your unveiling, final presentation).

It is a trial close that gives you a chance to see where any loyalties of the prospect's employees; that are involved, may be.

It is also your trial close regarding pricing. Final adjustments will be made after this meeting before you present your final quotation and ask for the order.

This is usually for a multi-page proposal for a larger order and there may be many your prospects employees' who will be present.

Inform them of the Reasons

It is best to discuss the reasons for this meeting with your main contact ahead of time for approval and to allow them to decide who should attend and when to have this meeting.

This should not be difficult to justify as you can present it as a beneficial meeting for them. It is to make sure you have everything they want. It is their own special preview.

- Explain that this is a final review before your actual proposal to make sure you have all the information correct.
- It also provides them with their final input before you finalize your design; product specifications and estimating *(say whatever makes sense).*

Explain that often at this point new information or requirements have surfaced and these facts can be discussed and incorporated before your final presentation is made.

This meeting allows them one last review to make sure nothing has been missed or there are not items included that should not be there.

Pricing

You should say that your price will be close; but it is still budgetary. There may be some changes and there is still some fine tuning to do.

For You - this will be your own testing of the waters for price.

There is also a possibility that your prospect's upper management will also be there if the size of order is significant, so they will need to know the type of meeting it will be.

This way it will not be a surprise and viewed as a waste of time by them.

You Do Not need to Upset anyone at this point

General Notes for the Meeting

It is often a good gesture to bring and provide coffee, other beverages and donuts for everyone as they arrive at the meeting; especially a morning one. Find out how many will attend.

Note: Check with your contact before arranging to bring the coffee and donuts, to make sure it is alright.

Correct Protocol

If you will be bringing people from your company to assist you, then it is important to establish that they follow the correct meeting protocol.

When doing your presentation, it is extremely important to have one person in control for the entire meeting!!

And that is YOU!

Not your Manager!

Not an Engineer or Supplier!

It is YOU!

Make sure all of those attending from your company understand the protocol. You decide who speaks and when. You can even provide a brief outline limiting what they are to say.

Do Not let them Take Over!

The Agenda

Suggested Components for this Meeting

Part 1 – The Introductions

Part 2– Your Findings and Summary of their Needs

Part 3 – Offerings, Features, Benefits and Solutions - Point form

Part 4 – Installation and Terms and Conditions

Part 5 – Questions and Answers

Part 6 - Break

Part 7 – Pricing Review

Part 8 – Summary (*Your Call to Action*)

Ten General Tips for Meeting

1. It is a good idea to provide an agenda c/w timeline
2. Point out that there will be several mini-questions and answer periods at the end of each segment and a larger one at the end of your presentation.
3. Start with the introductions and the reason for the preliminary meeting and then move into the main part of your presentation.
4. Structure the first minutes following the introductions for the most important parts.
5. These parts will include your overview point form outlining their needs and your solutions (your offerings).
6. This point form part of the presentation will be followed by a more detailed explanation of your offerings and review of terms and conditions.
7. Be prepared to accommodate any questions that do come up
8. Do not let the whole meeting become a question and answer meeting.
9. If there is a lot to cover that may take longer than 25 minutes, it might be an idea to do it in two parts.
10. Perhaps say you will be stopping part way through for a short Q & A.

End this First Main part with a Q&A

This is an appropriate time for a break especially if there is only the pricing summary information to follow.

Although there will be no final pricing at this point, this will be a very budgetary review of the financial package, payment schedule and your terms and conditions.

This will be an Unofficial Trial Close

For Key Personnel

If any key personnel from your prospects company are present, they may have set a time limit for attending the main presentation.

If they know approximately how long it will be until pricing is covered, they can decide if they wish to stay for the break and review pricing.

If upper management is present at this meeting, you should always provide them with the entire package including pricing for this trial run at the start of the meeting and explain again the concept of the meeting.

Go through your contact to do this and get permission.

Explain your timing for handing out pricing and terms and conditions to avoid premature discussion from them. They will fully understand the need to prevent a meeting, from getting out of control.

Benefits of a Q & A

- Discovery of those opposed to you, your company or your proposal (offerings)
- Able to ask questions of any skeptics
    - Publicly show their objections
    - Publicly solve them
    - By raising these issues publicly, you can avoid or at least minimize back room discussions and the sabotage of your quotation after you have gone.
- **Able to discover and respond to:**
    - Hidden animosity for your company
    - A hidden agenda and reasons that someone may have for promoting your competitor
- Able to Obtain information on other needs they desire that were not previously mentioned
- Often Exposes features that your competition is offering
- Often can indicate where you are positioned regarding price or preference.

Often an informal Q & A increases trust and credibility and is your best opportunity to re-position yourself for your final presentation.

The Break

The break can provide a time when you can speak with upper management if they decide to stay. **Ask your contact first.** Often management will leave the more detailed portion to others and will discuss these details including pricing separately with their own people later.

The Dress Rehearsal Details

Overview

We are now into the details of the main components of your meeting. We have broken the meeting into the eight parts.

It is best to keep these separated as components and show them separately on your agenda as listed except for the designated part 8 which you will just call Action Required or Summary.

The Eight Parts and What to do

Part 1 – The Introductions

- Provide a brief history of your Company.
- Ask in advance who they want to start the introductions.
- If you are starting:
  - Introduce your company members that are present and their functions as well as any key suppliers.
  - Then Introductions of Customers employees and their functions
  - **Note:** Their upper management can abstain if they wish

Part 2 – Customer Needs Review

- Provide a review of your findings to date in point form.
- Provide an outline of what you see as their needs, specifications or requirements from those meetings.
- Confirm these are what they are looking for.
- Ask if you have missed anything?
- Is there anything new that has been added?
- Has anything been removed or should be shown as an option

Wait for a Response

- If there are additional items, write them down.
- If items are no longer needed or part of the project, remove them
- Provide answers if you can.

- If you cannot provide complete answers say you will get back to them and provide the information prior to or in your final proposal whichever they prefer.

3) Your Offerings, Solutions and Benefits

- Provide your solutions, products, services, or equipment recommendations in point form.
- Supply any Drawings necessary for Clarity

4) Installation and Terms and Conditions

- Provide a description of the Installation (if any)
- Provide a review of your Terms and Conditions. (remember your built-in objections rebuttal)
- Open the meeting to Final Questions and Answers before the break.
- Provide your Detailed Support Information and Data
- Provide Full product or Service details and specifications.

Part 5 – Question and Answers

- Keep to the allotted time. This can get out of hand quickly.

Part 6 – Break

You might provide a light snack, coffee, donuts (depends on time of day - same as final presentation) check with your contact for approval first. During the Break is the time to hand out any budget pricing.

Part 7 – Budget Pricing

Provide copies to your contact and let them hand out to the others of their own choosing.

Let them control who is qualified as you do not want to place this information incorrectly.

This is the time to also provide a copy to give to upper management if they have not been in attendance.

Part 8– Summary (Your Call to Action)

Have we now addressed all their needs?

What changes are required?

Re-state what additions have occurred?

Re-state what can be eliminated?

How do we look?

Suggested Meeting Guide

Preparation

- Set up and test any equipment being used in your presentation prior to your meeting.
- Ask for perhaps 10 to 15 minutes ahead of your meeting start time for this.
- Set out coffee and snacks.
- When people arrive for a meeting – some will agree with the reason for the meeting, some are agitated and feel it is a waste of their time.
- There may be background issues internal conflicts some are less enthused, and many will doubt you.

This informal 10 to 15-minute set-up time, and providing the coffee and snacks is invaluable for breaking the ice and easing tensions and opposition.

The Time Allotted

Make your initial agenda time line to suit the original time they have provided for you. We have provided the example of 60 to 72-minute timeline.

Make your agenda time line scalable. Show the times you have allowed for each part of your agenda. This makes the prospect aware of what will take palace and how long you have allowed for each part.

If they decide to extend any part of the agenda, they will also realize what happens to the time line.

Tell them your plan and give them the option to expand any area that the feel needs more time to cover. They can change the time but do not just let things get out of control or you will be rushed at the end.

The 60 to 72 Minute Time Line

Part 1 – Opening Introductions	4 to 5 minutes
Part 2 – Needs	7 to 8 minutes
Part 3 – Offerings and Solutions	11 to 12 minutes
Part 4 - Terms and Conditions	8 to 10 minutes
Sub Total Parts 1 to 4	**30 to 35 minutes**
Part 5 - Questions and Answers	6 to 8 minutes
Part 6 - Break – Informal Q&A -	10 to 12 minutes
Part 7 - Pricing	9 to 10 minutes
Part 8 – Summary (Call to Action)	5 to 7 minutes
Sub Total Parts 5 to 8	**30 to 37 minutes**
Total Meeting	**60 to 72 minutes**

Summary of the Dress Rehearsal

By making the prime message of your meeting a point form presentation you will be able to deliver a clear communication that is easily understood and fully absorbed.

- The greatest danger that can occur is to get totally bogged down in too much unnecessary detail in your initial part of your presentation and lose the clarity of your message.
- This will confuse the reasons why they should choose you.
- It is essential that you capture and maintain the client's interest during all parts.
- If you do this correctly, your prospect will want to take part in the discussions and be anxious to hear your final proposal.

There is usually more than one meeting for a large project or large piece of equipment and the dress rehearsal is a critical one.

Your client will usually want to review the details of this one as well, before having the final meeting.

This part is Considered the Appetizer

If you have Presented

Evaluation

It is here; when you are finished, that you will get a reaction to your solutions and equipment concepts.

If you have provided a budget price you can also get a reaction to this as well which will allow you to have another check point to gauge your position and chances to obtain the order.

You are now ready with all the facts to start the assembly of your final presentation.

THE FINAL PRESENTATION

The Overview

How to Assemble the Final Presentation

It is time to put your final presentation together for the order. Your dress rehearsal should have provided all the missing and key components from your discussion and possibly uncovered some decision-making tips.

You can now proceed with more confidence in what your client is looking for.

What comes first?

- Price or Solutions and Benefits?
- The customer always wants price.
- It should always be – Solutions and benefits.

Why Solutions and Benefits first?

Pricing is often the first place in a proposal that people will turn to (if it is available) especially when you are making your final quotation.

If you have pricing as part of your main proposal package they may disengage immediately from your explanation of Solutions and Benefits.

Why Pricing Comes Last

If pricing is presented first:

- There has been no explanation of what is included in the price.
- There is no justification for the Price yet.
- No solutions have been discussed.
- No benefits have been discussed.
- Terms and Conditions have not been discussed.
- What is included has not been outlined.

Result

All they see is the Price and there may be total justification if your price is higher.

- It may have a lot more benefits with a better Return on their investment
- Your quality may be higher
- Your delivery may be better
- You may include more things in your terms and conditions or installation than your competitor

All these benefits could be lost because you have not been able to show them first and show value.

People will be Thinking only of the Price

And Not the Value

If the Price is Presented First

It is important to be able to provide a description of your main features, benefits and solutions to meet their needs; before you cover the pricing aspect, or there is no value perceived to justify the price that is provided.

This is very important to remember and is one of the main reasons to keep pricing separate from the rest of the package. It needs to be handed out at the appropriate time and to the right people.

There will always be pressure to go to pricing first. Stand your ground and leave pricing until later or you may ***"Pay the Price."***

If you prepare your contact properly and establish your procedure right from the beginning, there should not be a problem.

Suggested Meeting Components

Part 1 – The Introductions

Part 2– Summary of their Needs

Part 3 – Your Offerings, Features, Benefits and Solutions

Part 4 – Questions and Answers

Part 5 – Break (snacks, coffee, tea or soft drinks)

Part 6 – Installation Responsibilities, Terms and Conditions

Part 7 – Short Q & A part 6

Part 8 – Pricing (Equipment and Installation), ROI, Incentives

Part 9 – Final Q & A

Part10 – Summary (your Call to Action)

The Meeting Details

Overview

We are now into the main components of your Final Presentation Meeting. We have broken the meeting into the ten main parts shown above.

It is best that you treat these main parts as totally separate components and show them separately on your agenda as well.

Part 10 on the agenda you hand out is labeled

Summary - Not Call to Action

Respect for their Management

If any key personnel from the customer are present, they may have set a time limit for attending the main presentation.

If they know how long your meeting will be, they can decide how long they will need to stay to hear an important part.

You should always immediately provide upper management (through your contact) with the total presentation package including agenda and all parts including pricing, ROI and their terms and conditions.

Explain the Approach

You should explain that in your normal presentation process you cover the total package, the benefits and solutions and terms and conditions first before presenting price so that the pricing makes sense.

If they stay for the Entire Presentation

That is Good

The break can provide a time when you can speak with upper management if they decide to stay. Go through your contact.

Pricing is also best to come next after the break.

This allows those people who have a say in the product and any applicable terms and conditions (but do not get involved in pricing) to take part in the break and food and informal Q&A.

In this way, they will not feel excluded. They will be more likely to become a supportive friend behind the scenes.

The Meeting

Who should you Bring?

As the potential new suppler, you also may want to have a few of your own people there to assist you. Perhaps your management; engineering or service personnel will be there to answer questions.

Possibly bring key suppliers that may be part of your proposal package.

Rules of behavior

It is critical that all those attending including suppliers and everyone from your company including your managers fully understand that there is only one person in charge of the meeting and that person is you.

They may speak only when called upon by you or asked by the prospect. They will say their part and immediately turn the meeting back to you when they are done by saying your name.

This must be a totally agreed upon fact before anyone attends the meeting. (Including your superiors)

Note: Have a "Pre-Presentation" meeting with your support group to cover everything including this protocol.

Often others; especially your managers or engineering, may want to take over the limelight once they get started.

1) It should be an absolute rule that it is **"Not Allowed"**
2) You are to be totally in charge from start to finish
3) If you (as the sales person) lose control of the meeting; *"as the authority figure"*, you are doomed when it comes to asking for the order or controlling this part.

Lesson Learned

- I learned this the hard way with meetings disrupted by overzealous engineers, suppliers and even my manager.
- The client began directing all further questions to these support people who: for the most part, were not qualified to ask for the order or answer objections.
- The entire sales process was out of control and it became extremely difficult to regain my position as the authority figure to get the sale.
- Do not let this happen, or you may be leaving without an order.

The Agenda

Part 1 – The Introductions

- Ask in advance who they want to start the introductions.
- If it is you,
  - Introduce your company members that are present and their functions, followed by Suppliers and description of their involvement.
  - Then Introductions of Customers employees and their functions.
  - **Note:** Their upper management can abstain if they wish.

Presentation Start

Part 2 – Needs

What to do

- **As a last-minute detail, the day before your meeting,** you will have called and asked your contact if there is anything new or if there are there any last-minute changes because of your final review meeting, and make any adjustments required.

Point Form will be noted below as (PF)

- Provide a review of your findings during your earlier meetings. (PF) = Point Form
- Do a quick review of their needs, specifications or requirements from those meetings and confirm these are what they are still looking for. (PF)
- Include and mention any changes that occurred because of your Dress Rehearsal. Ask if anything else has been added or if anything has changed since your last conversations.

- You should be clear to continue; but, surprises can occur. Be ready to handle them and make the changes to your final package while you are there.

Part 3 - Your Recommendations

- Provide a point form summary of your offerings, solutions and benefits.
- Supply any Drawings or visual aids necessary for Clarity.

Use PowerPoint, slides, literature or drawings. Be very thorough and cover all the important areas.

Part 4 - Questions and Answer Session

Here you will also control the meeting and you will either answer the questions asked or designate one of your company members or suppliers to answer it, if they are better suited.

Again, they should do their part and turn the meeting back over to you by verbally saying your name. *"Back to You (your name)"*

Part 5 - Break – Use this time also for an extended informal Q & A. It is also mingling time and opportunities for multiple discussions.

Keep this part under control and a maximum time as outlined or you will lose control and be unable to get the momentum going again easily.

Wherever the meeting is taking place you will have made proper arrangements for the food part in advance.

Menu Suggestions

a) **Start of the day** - Have coffee, tea, soft drinks and water. Provide donuts or an alternative healthier fruit snack.

b) **Mid-morning or midafternoon** keep it simple: a cheese tray, cold meats, bread, and cold drinks

c) **Lunch** – Sandwiches, veggie or cheese platter, cold meats and bread, coffee, soft drinks, cookies or treats (discuss with your contact)

d) **Afternoon** – Same as Mid-Morning

Part 6 - Installation and Terms and Conditions

At this point you will review Installation (if any) along with terms and conditions which are usually tied very closely to any installation.

Have a point form description of the installation for quick review.

Have a detailed description of Installation as backup support

Have your terms and conditions relating to the project clearly defined and show everything that you have included and what is not included. (remember your built-in condition rebuttal)

Often the terms and conditions can make the difference in getting an order or losing it. Your competition may have left out costly items that you have included that might be overlooked.

Part 7 – Questions and Answer for Part 6

Be prepared as this can easily get out of control. State at the beginning the time that you have allowed for this part.

If asked any questions, make sure your support team does not take over the meeting. Have a clear understanding of who is in charge.

Part 8 - Provide Pricing

Your Q & A has ended and once the non-attendees for the pricing part have left continue.

1. Financial Information
    a. Equipment and Installation Pricing
    b. Optional Prices
    c. Payment schedule
    d. ROI, Information
    e. Incentives available
2. Provide your Terms and Conditions relating to pricing
3. Provide any Testimonials that are relevant
4. Having some good pictures and visual aids can increase the perception of value.
5. Have charts showing pricing details, incentives, leasing rates, Options and ROI.

Break your pricing summary into components by providing as many options with add-on pricing as possible. This way they feel they have control and your base price will look better as well.

By providing options separately you give the client control over any extra costs for added benefits.

In this way, you can discuss the benefits and features of the options and add-on to show the added value for each of them.

If it is Applicable and Results are good, show any ROI for any Options as well

End of Formal Presentation

Part 9 – Final Questions and Answers for Everything

Part 10 – Summary (Your Call to action - Closing

- Ask for the order using the appropriate closing method.
- Answer any objections using the 5 Step process.
- Usually you will get only get an indication of your chances to get the order; but if you do get one, Thank them for the Order.

Meeting Time Lines

Set up and test any equipment such as projectors or sound systems that are being used for your presentation. Do this prior to your meeting. Ask for perhaps 15 – 20 minutes ahead of your meeting start time for this. Set out the coffee and donuts first.

When people arrive for a meeting

Some are emotional, some are glad to take part, some may be agitated, some are enthusiastic others may be complacent.

There may be background issues internal conflicts some are less enthused, and many may not know you and will doubt you.

This informal 10 – 15-minute time with coffee and donuts while you are getting set up is invaluable for breaking the ice and easing tensions and opposition.

The Breakdown

Make your agenda time line scalable. Show the times you have allowed for each part of your agenda. Make sure the prospect is aware of what will take palace and how long you have allowed for it.

If they decide to extend any part of the agenda, they will also realize what happens to the time line. Tell them your plan and give them the option to expand any area that the feel needs more time to cover.

The 72 to 90 Minute Time Line

Sample Time Line – Adjust to suit	
Part 1 – Introductions -	1 to 3 minutes
Actual Presentation Begins	
Part 2 – Their Needs	10 to 12 minutes
Part 3 – Your Offerings, Features Benefits -	12 to 14 minutes
Part 4 – Questions and Answers First Half -	**5 to 6 minutes**
Total time Parts 1 to 4	**28 to 35 minutes**
Part 5 - BREAK –	8 to 9 minutes
Presentation Continues	
Part 6 – Installation Duties, Terms & Conditions	10 to 12 minutes
Part 7 – Short Q & A for 6	2 to 4 minutes
Part 8 – Pricing, ROI, Incentives -	14 to 16 minutes
Total time Parts 6 to 8	**26 to 32 minutes**
Part 9 – Final Questions and Answers	5 to 7 minutes
Part 10 – Summary (Call to Action)	5 to 7 minutes
Total time Parts 9& 10	**10 to 14 minutes**
Total meeting time line including Break –	**72 to 90 minutes**

Summary of the Final Presentation

Trial Closings

Throughout the meeting, you will be asking things like:

- Is that right?
- Is that what you wanted?
- How are we doing so far?
- Does that solve the problem?

These questions are very helpful to see if your presentation is on track and may prevent surprises at the end of it.

Whenever pricing is discussed, you must always ask how you look as a minimum requirement with an expectation of a response.

Asking for the sale is what this is all about and your closes will help you get the order.

Make Your Best Effort to Close

Ultimately, you may need to leave it with the decision makers, to discuss before they give you a final answer.

Asking how you look, will (if answered) provide a strong indication of where you stand and could give you another chance if you are not solidly in there.

Leaving it for a final decision is often the case on large purchases so you should not panic if this happens.

Our Part 2 on Qualifying and Closing has provided many ways to ask for the order while you are there.

Our part 3 Overcoming Objections will provide you with the necessary information for completion of the sale.

Extra Time

Because this is a final presentation the length for any part could be even longer.

It is important to take a short break approximately every 20 to 25 minutes. After 25 minutes the attention is much lower and sometimes not there at all.

We have already discussed making your time line scalable and showing allotted times on your agenda. Leave it open but ask the prospect if any area needs to be extended

THE CALL BACK MEETING

The call back is when you have left without a sale after your earlier final presentation. There may have been a reason or condition why you could not proceed at that time, or maybe you were just not good enough to close that day.

Other reasons:

- There may have been areas for you to re-consider or re-structure in your quotation
- They could have needed to talk to someone else or wait for more quotes to come in.
- They needed time to think it over or discuss it with all their people involved.
- Perhaps the Main Decision Maker wants to see you one more time before they decide.

Now any Previous Conditions have been met

- You have reviewed your presentation and made any requested changes.
- You have called to arrange your Appointment

If No Changes Were Requested

Find out how much time they will be setting aside for your meeting, who will be attending and how many copies they will need. The answers that they provide to these questions will often reveal what your chances will be.

Be Totally Prepared

- To Answer any Questions about the Project
- To Ask for the Order
- To Answer any Objections

If Changes Were Requested

If changes were requested, inform them that you have made them, and are looking forward to showing these improvements to them.

Use the Word Improvements

Do Not Call Them Changes

People Hate Changes

1. Make sure that you have followed these steps before your visit,
    a. Prepare your new proposal so that it is up to date.
    b. Make sure your agenda fits the time allotted for your visit.
    c. Provide the right number of copies plus some to spare.
    d. Tag any areas in your proposal that have (changed) been improved with a removable sticker.
2. Prepare a list in point form of the (changes) improvements that you have made and all the areas you want to discuss during your visit.
3. Leave some space between each item in your review copy so that you can write down any additional comments.
4. Put it on your letterhead, and you can even call it "Appendix A" or something appropriate. You may want to attach it to your quote or use it as such.

When you arrive:

"You thank the prospect for seeing you again."

Then you say:

"So that I do not take up more time than you have set aside, I have prepared a summary of your main concerns that we discussed on my last visit or (our last telephone conversation)."

"I have made a copy for you so that we can review these areas quickly together."

"I have also revised our proposal to reflect those improvements and placed these removable stickers in each location of the revision."

If they are Receptive

Do not rush through your presentation like a runaway freight train. Confirm again how much time they have set aside and begin your presentation.

You have already asked how much time they are setting aside, who will be there and how many copies they will want.

Hand them your Agenda with Time Line

Start reviewing the changes (improvements). If questions are asked, provide your answers. After each item, ask if they need more clarification, or if that satisfies their concern and/or meets their needs.

Go through the whole proposal and when you finish, you ask if there are any new areas that may have developed since your last conversation.

If there are No Additions or Changes Required

Ask again if today's meeting has answered all their questions and concerns.

If they say Yes

Choose your Appropriate Close

And

CLOSE IT!

If there are Additional Changes

Address them and make every effort to solve them when you are there. If you leave them unanswered, you could lose any further opportunity to get the sale.

If they are major changes then you will need to arrange to come back with the new changes if they are willing for another **Call Back.**

SUMMARY

The greatest satisfaction in perfecting presentation skills is that you will have optimum control over the potential outcome of your sales efforts.

You will have confidence in knowing that you have a plan, a track to run on and a way to obtain the greatest leverage for achieving the sale.

You will have the upper hand by knowing exactly where your presentations are headed and that you are in control.

You are now equipped to make any of the different types of presentations that you will need.

END OF PART FOUR

Wayne E Shillum – Author

www.ingramcontent.com/pod-product-compliance
Ingram Content Group UK Ltd.
Pitfield, Milton Keynes, MK11 3LW, UK
UKHW051129260726
13967UKWH00010B/2947

9 781987 978131